AUSTRALIA: HUMAN RIGHTS

EXECUTIVE SUMMARY

Australia is a constitutional democracy with a freely elected federal parliamentary government. In free and fair federal parliamentary elections held in September, the Liberal Party and National Party coalition won a majority in the 150-seat House of Representatives and formed a government with Tony Abbott as prime minister. Authorities maintained effective control over the security forces. Security forces did not commit human rights abuses.

The main human rights problems reported were domestic violence against women and children, particularly in indigenous communities; discrimination against indigenous people; and policies affecting asylum seekers, including lengthy detention and austere detention center conditions for some arriving to Australia by sea.

The government took steps to prosecute officials accused of abuses, and ombudsmen, human rights bodies, and internal government mechanisms responded effectively to complaints.

Section 1. Respect for the Integrity of the Person, Including Freedom from:

a. Arbitrary or Unlawful Deprivation of Life

There were no reports that the government or its agents committed arbitrary or unlawful killings.

b. Disappearance

There were no reports of politically motivated disappearances.

c. Torture and Other Cruel, Inhuman, or Degrading Treatment or Punishment

The law prohibits such practices, and the government generally respected these provisions. There were occasional reports that police and prison officials mistreated suspects in custody. Some indigenous groups asserted that harassment of indigenous persons and racial discrimination by some police and prison custodians persisted.

Prison and Detention Center Conditions

Prison and detention center conditions generally met international standards, including access to potable water, and the government permitted visits by independent human rights observers.

Physical Conditions: According to the Australian Bureau of Statistics (ABS), from March to June the average number of inmates in prison custody countrywide (excluding persons in community-based and other minimum-security facilities) was 30,812, including 2,346 women and 7,659 unsentenced inmates. Unsentenced inmates included pretrial detainees, convicted prisoners awaiting sentencing, and persons awaiting deportation. According to the Productivity Commission, in 2010-11 prison utilization was 101 percent of prison design capacity. In August the ombudsman in the state of Victoria reported that overcrowding in that state's prisons was likely to worsen and present a risk for those detained and for the state as a custodian. In October the Australian Services Union warned that prisons in the state of Queensland were becoming overcrowded.

In May the Australian Institute of Criminology reported that there were 58 deaths in prison from July 2010 through June 2011, 12 (21 percent) of which were of indigenous persons. The annual rate of death for indigenous prisoners was 0.16 per 100 compared with 0.22 per 100 for nonindigenous prisoners. Of the 12 indigenous deaths, eight were from natural causes, three from suicide, and one from other causes.

A number of domestic and international human rights groups voiced concerns about conditions at immigration detention centers (see section 2.d.).

Administration: Recordkeeping on prisoners was adequate. Both federal and state governments funded "juvenile diversion" programs to keep young persons out of the court and prison systems. Federal, state, and territorial government ombudsmen can serve on behalf of prisoners and detainees to consider such matters as alternatives to incarceration for nonviolent offenders; addressing the status and circumstances of confinement of juvenile offenders; and improving pretrial detention, bail, and recordkeeping procedures. Prisoners and detainees had access to visitors, could observe religious practices, and could submit complaints to government-funded legal aid offices; federal, state, and territorial ombudsmen; and judicial authorities without censorship. Authorities investigated allegations of inhuman conditions and documented the results of such investigations in a publicly accessible manner. The government investigated and monitored prison and detention center conditions.

d. Arbitrary Arrest or Detention

The law prohibits arbitrary arrest and detention, and the government observed these prohibitions.

Role of the Police and Security Apparatus

The armed forces, under the minister for defense, are responsible for external security. The Australian Federal Police (AFP), under the minister for home affairs and justice, and state and territorial police forces are responsible for internal security. The AFP enforces national laws, and state and territorial police forces enforce state and territorial laws. Civilian authorities maintained effective control over the armed forces and police, and the government has effective mechanisms to investigate and punish abuse and corruption. There were no reports of impunity involving the security forces during the year.

Arrest Procedures and Treatment of Detainees

Police officers may seek an arrest warrant from a magistrate when a suspect cannot be located or fails to appear; however, they also may arrest a person without a warrant if there are reasonable grounds to believe the person committed an offense. Police must inform arrested persons immediately of their legal rights and the grounds for their arrest, and arrested persons must be brought before a magistrate for a bail hearing at the next sitting of the court. The law, however, permits police to hold individuals in preventive detention for up to 24 hours without charge if a senior police official finds it is "reasonably necessary to prevent a terrorist act or preserve evidence of such an act." Individuals may be detained for an additional 24 hours under court order.

The law states that the maximum investigation period for which a person may be held and questioned without charge is 24 hours, unless extended by court order. In the case of a terrorism suspect, however, the law establishes a seven-day limit on the total amount of time the suspect can be held if the questioning is spread over several days.

A separate provision of law permits the attorney general to grant the Australian Security Intelligence Organization (ASIO) authority to detain a person for a continuous period of up to 168 hours in special circumstances, such as "reasonable grounds for believing that issuing the warrant to be requested will substantially assist the collection of intelligence that is important in relation to a terrorism offense." ASIO, however, had not used this authority as of year's end.

The law permits a judge to authorize "control orders" on individuals suspected of involvement with terrorism-related activities. These orders may include a range of measures, such as monitoring of suspects and house arrest, and may be in effect for up to a year without the filing of criminal charges. If a control order remains warranted after one year, a new court order must be sought.

By law there is an independent monitor to help ensure that counterterrorism laws strike an appropriate balance between protecting the community and protecting human rights. Both the Australian Federal Police Commission and the Australian Crime Commission are subject to parliamentary oversight.

Bail generally is available to persons facing criminal charges unless the person is considered to be a flight risk or is charged with an offense carrying a penalty of 12 months' imprisonment or more. Attorneys and families were granted prompt access to detainees. Government-provided attorneys are available to give legal advice to detainees who cannot afford counsel. Arrested persons enjoy additional legal protections, such as the ability to challenge the lawfulness of a detention and apply for compensation if unlawfully detained.

Detention of Rejected Asylum Seekers or Stateless Persons: A small number of asylum seekers remained in long-term detention despite having exhausted the appeal process; they could not be returned to their home country because they lacked travel documents or could not obtain necessary transit visas.

e. Denial of Fair Public Trial

The law provides for an independent judiciary, and the government respected judicial independence.

Trial Procedures

The law provides for the right to a fair trial, and an independent judiciary generally enforced this right. In the state district and county courts, and the state and territorial supreme courts, there generally is a judge and jury for serious offenses. The judge conducts the trial, and the jury decides on the facts and renders the verdict. Defendants enjoy the presumption of innocence and cannot be compelled to testify or confess guilt. They have the right to be informed promptly and in detail of the charges, with free interpretation as necessary, and the right to an attorney and adequate time and facilities to prepare a defense. Government-funded attorneys are available to low-income persons. The defendant's attorney can question witnesses, present witnesses and evidence, access relevant government-held evidence, and appeal the court's decision or the sentence imposed.

Political Prisoners and Detainees

There were no reports of political prisoners or detainees.

Civil Judicial Procedures and Remedies

There is an independent and impartial judiciary in civil matters, and individuals or organizations may seek civil judicial remedies for human rights violations. There is also an administrative process at the state and federal levels to seek redress for alleged wrongs by government departments. Administrative tribunals may review a government decision only if the decision is in a category specified under a law, regulation, or other legislative instrument as subject to a tribunal's review.

f. Arbitrary Interference with Privacy, Family, Home, or Correspondence

The law prohibits such actions, and the government effectively enforced these prohibitions. Police have authority to enter premises without a warrant in emergency circumstances.

Section 2. Respect for Civil Liberties, Including:

a. Freedom of Speech and Press

Although the constitution does not explicitly provide for freedom of speech or press, the High Court has held that a right to freedom of expression is implied in the constitution, and the government generally respected these rights. An independent press, an effective judiciary, and a functioning democratic political system combined to promote freedom of speech and press.

Internet Freedom

There were no government restrictions on access to the internet or credible reports that the government monitored e-mail or internet chat rooms without appropriate legal authority. The internet was widely available to and used by citizens. According to the International Telecommunication Union, 82 percent of the population used the internet in 2012.

Law enforcement agencies require a warrant to intercept telecommunications, including internet communications. In emergency situations the director general of ASIO may issue a warrant for this purpose without prior judicial authorization, but the attorney general must be informed.

The Australian Communications and Media Authority (ACMA) maintained a list of so-called refused classification website content, primarily pertaining to child pornography, sexual violence, and other activities illegal in the country, compiled as a result of a consumer complaints process. ACMA may issue a notice to the provider to remove domestically hosted "refused classification" material, or links to such material, that is the subject of such a complaint if an investigation concludes the complaint is justified. The list is available to providers of filtering software. An owner or operator of such a website can appeal an ACMA decision to the Administrative Appeals Tribunal. Since 2010 three major telecommunications providers have voluntarily blocked websites on Interpol's list of child-abuse links.

Academic Freedom and Cultural Events

There were no government restrictions on academic freedom or cultural events.

b. Freedom of Peaceful Assembly and Association

While the rights of peaceful assembly and association are not codified in law, the government generally respected these rights.

c. Freedom of Religion

See the Department of State's *International Religious Freedom Report* at www.state.gov/j/drl/irf/rpt/.

d. Freedom of Movement, Internally Displaced Persons, Protection of Refugees, and Stateless Persons

The law provides for freedom of internal movement, foreign travel, emigration, and repatriation, and the government generally respected these rights. The government cooperated with the Office of the UN High Commissioner for Refugees (UNHCR) and other humanitarian organizations in providing protection and assistance to internally displaced persons, refugees, returning refugees, asylum seekers, stateless persons, and other persons of concern.

Protection of Refugees

Access to Asylum: The country's laws provide for the granting of asylum or refugee status, and the government has established a system for providing protection to refugees.

The number of asylum seekers arriving by sea significantly increased in recent years, putting pressure on detention center capacity and processing times. In the 2012-13 fiscal year, 25,750 such arrivals were recorded, compared with 25 in 2007-08. Under third-party arrangements restarted in 2012, the government sent asylum seekers to Nauru and Papua New Guinea for processing of refugee status determinations and resettlement. Due to processing backlogs, the government granted some new asylum seekers "bridging visas" permitting them to live in the community because it was not possible to process all new asylum seekers offshore.

The law authorizes the immigration minister to designate a country a regional offshore processing center by regulation, if the minister determines it is in the national interest to do so, and requires the minister to notify parliament, which may then disapprove the proposed designation within five working days of notification. The law states that such a designation "need not be limited by reference to the international obligations or domestic law of that country." Under the government's policy on asylum processing for unauthorized maritime arrivals, asylum seekers transferred to third countries for regional processing will have their asylum claims assessed by the country in which the claim is processed. The immigration minister stated in 2012 that asylum seekers processed in Nauru and Papua New Guinea would not be entitled to judicial review of their cases under Australian law but would be entitled to a merit-based review in the processing country.

In July the former government entered into a Regional Resettlement Arrangement (RRA) with Papua New Guinea to send all unauthorized maritime arrivals to Papua New Guinea for assessment and to resettle those found to be refugees in Papua New Guinea. In August Nauru became part of the arrangement. The government began transferring all unauthorized maritime asylum seeker arrivals to Papua New Guinea and Nauru for processing.

On July 12, the UNHCR released a report on the Manus Island Regional Processing Centre (RPC) in Papua New Guinea, finding that while there were improvements since its last mission to the RPC, the arrangements still did not meet international protection standards for the reception and treatment of asylum seekers. The report stated that progress had been made regarding the legal framework for processing and acknowledged that some improvements had been made to the physical settings at the RPC, although it described the living conditions as "still harsh." The government pledged to work with the UNHCR to address concerns with the RPC while it continued to build a permanent facility on Manus Island slated for completion in 2014. Subsequent to the announcement of the RRA, the UNHCR said it was troubled by the absence of adequate protection standards and safeguards for asylum seekers and refugees in Papua New Guinea. The UNHCR expressed its concern that "sustainable integration of non-Melanesian refugees in the socioeconomic and cultural life of Papua New Guinea will raise formidable challenges."

The Department of Immigration and Citizenship provided immigration advice and assistance to persons making an initial asylum claim or application for lawful residence, but the government announced in September it would stop providing taxpayer-funded legal assistance to asylum seekers. There is a statutory obligation to facilitate access to legal representation for persons in immigration detention.

On May 21, the Commonwealth Ombudsman reported that there were 11 deaths in immigration detention between July 2010 and April 2013: four suicides, two due to natural causes; four coroner's investigations not finalized; and an April 2013 death that remained under police investigation. The ombudsman found "a strong correlation between the rise in the average time in detention and the increase in self-harming behavior during 2011" and a significant decrease in the rate of self-harm after October 2011 when asylum seekers were granted bridging visas to reside in the community while their asylum claims were being processed. The ombudsman recommended prioritizing the processing of cases of detainees who have been detained for the longest period, and for the Department of Immigration and Citizenship to continue "to review and improve health and mental health standards in accordance with state, territory, and national standards."

Delays in processing asylum applications resulted in protracted detention of some asylum seekers. The commonwealth ombudsman reviews all cases of persons in detention for two years or more. As of June 26, there were 399 persons in immigration detention longer than two years. The government stated that asylum seekers in Nauru could wait up to five years for their applications to be processed based on the "no advantage" principle that those arriving by boat be processed according to the same timeline as other asylum seekers. In July a riot by asylum seekers detained in Nauru overwhelmed authorities and caused an estimated Australian dollar (A$) 60 million ($55.8 million) in damages to the detention facility before local community members were able to assist police in restoring order.

In August the UN Human Rights Committee raised concerns regarding the treatment of 46 refugees held in detention on security grounds and called for their release. Australia deemed the refugees a security risk and at year's end had held them in immigration detention for at least 30 months.

According to media, between July 1 and September 6, the government approved the transfer to group homes of 409 children who were in mainland immigration detention.

Refoulement: In law and practice the government provided protection against the expulsion or return of refugees to countries where their lives or freedom would be threatened on account of their race, religion, nationality, membership in a particular social group, or political opinion.

In March a group of members of Afghanistan's parliament urged the Australian government not to return 125 Hazara asylum seekers to Afghanistan. On March 21, the federal court ruled that an Afghan asylum seeker, due to be deported to Kabul, had not had a fair hearing. Asylum seeker advocates claimed that he would be killed if returned to Afghanistan. The case continued as of November.

Durable Solutions: The government accepted refugees for resettlement from third countries and funded refugee resettlement services, such as language and employment programs.

Section 3. Respect for Political Rights: The Right of Citizens to Change Their Government

The constitution and law provide citizens the right to change their government peacefully, and citizens exercised this right through periodic, free, and fair elections based on universal suffrage and mandatory voting.

Elections and Political Participation

Recent Elections: The country held free and fair federal parliamentary elections on September 7. The Liberal-National Party Coalition defeated the Labor government, and Tony Abbott replaced Kevin Rudd as prime minister. The coalition won 90 seats in the 150-seat House of Representatives, the Labor Party 55, and others five.

Participation of Women and Minorities: There are no legal impediments to public office for women or minorities. Following the September 7 election, there were 68 women in the 226-seat federal parliament (39 in the House of Representatives and 29 in the Senate). The prime minister (until June 27), the governor-general, and the speaker of the house were women. There were three female judges on the seven-member High Court. After the election there was one female minister in the 19-member federal cabinet, four women among the 11 ministers outside the cabinet, and one woman among the 12 parliamentary secretaries. There was one woman among the eight premiers and chief ministers of the six states and two territories.

Indigenous persons and other minorities generally were underrepresented among the political leadership relative to their share of the population. In 2010 an indigenous person was elected to the federal House of Representatives for the first time, and the first indigenous person was elected to the Senate in September. There were two indigenous persons in the Western Australia State parliament and six in the Northern Territory legislative assembly. The Tasmania and New South Wales state parliaments and the Australian Capital Territory legislative assembly each had one indigenous member.

Section 4. Corruption and Lack of Transparency in Government

The law provides criminal penalties for corruption by officials, and the government generally implemented these laws effectively.

Corruption: There were isolated reports of government corruption during the year. The AFP had initiated bribery-related charges against nine men in connection with efforts from 1999 to 2005 to secure banknote contracts in Malaysia, Indonesia, and Vietnam on behalf of a company then half owned by the Reserve Bank of Australia. In August 2012 one of the men was sentenced to six months' imprisonment and suspended for two years after pleading guilty and agreeing to provide evidence in the investigation.

Queensland, Western Australia, and New South Wales states have anticorruption bodies that investigate alleged government corruption, and every jurisdiction has an ombudsman who investigates and makes recommendations in response to complaints about government decisions. These bodies actively collaborated with civil society, operated independently and effectively, and had adequate resources.

Whistleblower Protection: The law provides protection to public and private employees who make internal disclosures or lawful public disclosures of evidence of illegality. The law was implemented effectively to protect whistleblowers from retaliation. The government passed the Public Interest Disclosure Bill of 2013 to encourage the disclosure of wrongdoing within the public service and strengthen protections for public service whistleblowers.

Financial Disclosure: The law requires all federal, state, and territory elected officials to report their financial interests. Failure to do so would result in a finding of contempt of parliament and punitive measures. Federal officeholders must report their financial interests to a Register of Pecuniary Interests, which is made public within 28 days of the individual's assumption of office.

Public Access to Information: Federal, state, and territorial governments have freedom of information (FOI) laws that provide the public with access to government information; some charge application and processing fees. The federal government does not charge application fees. Government information may be exempted from disclosure to protect essential public interests or the private or business affairs of others. An applicant, including foreign media, may appeal a government decision to deny a request for information to the quasi-legal Administrative Appeals Tribunal, an executive body that reviews administrative decisions by government entities. An adverse Administrative Appeals Tribunal decision may be appealed to the Federal Court. FOI laws, including appeal mechanisms, generally functioned effectively. A government initiated review of FOI laws released on August 2 recommended "the exemption for cabinet documents be clarified" and that "no charge should be payable for the first five hours of processing time."

A FOI commissioner is responsible for promoting and protecting information rights.

Section 5. Governmental Attitude Regarding International and Nongovernmental Investigation of Alleged Violations of Human Rights

A wide variety of domestic and international human rights groups generally operated without government restriction, investigating and publishing their findings on human rights cases. Government officials often were cooperative and responsive to their views.

Government Human Rights Bodies: The Human Rights Commission (HRC), which is independent and adequately funded by the federal government, investigates complaints of discrimination or breaches of human rights under the federal laws that implement the country's human rights treaty obligations. The media and nongovernmental organizations (NGOs) deemed its reports accurate and reported them widely. Parliament has a Joint Committee on Human Rights, and federal law requires that a statement of compatibility with international human rights obligations accompany each new bill.

In addition to the HRC at the federal level, each state and territory has a human rights ombudsman.

Section 6. Discrimination, Societal Abuses, and Trafficking in Persons

Federal laws prohibit discrimination based on disability, race, color, descent or national or ethnic origin, marital status, age, gender, gender identity, sexual orientation, and intersex status. An independent judiciary and a network of federal, state, and territorial equal opportunity offices effectively enforced antidiscrimination laws.

Women

Rape and Domestic Violence: The law criminalizes rape, including spousal rape, and the government enforced the law effectively when cases were reported to authorities. The laws of the individual states and territories prescribe the penalties for rape.

The law prohibits violence against women, including domestic abuse, and the government enforced the law. Violence against women remained a problem, particularly in indigenous communities.

According to the 2005 ABS Personal Safety Survey (the latest available), one in three women had experienced physical violence since the age of 15, and almost one in five experienced sexual violence. The ABS reported that during 2012, police recorded 15,137 victims of sexual assault, 83 percent of whom were women.

Observers believed domestic violence to be substantially underreported, particularly in indigenous communities; among reasons cited for this were cultural factors and the isolation of many indigenous communities. The federal and state governments funded programs to combat domestic violence and support victims, including the funding of numerous women's shelters. Police received training in responding to domestic violence. Federal, state, and territorial governments collaborated on the National Plan to Reduce Violence Against Women and their Children 2010-22, which is the first effort to coordinate action at all levels of government to reduce the levels of violence against women.

Sexual Harassment: The law prohibits sexual harassment. Complaints of such harassment can lead to criminal proceedings or disciplinary action against the defendant and compensation claims by the plaintiff. Complaints of sexual harassment as well as sex discrimination may be submitted to the HRC under the Sex Discrimination Act. The HRC received 215 complaints of sexual harassment from July 2012 to June, but separate statistics on resolution of harassment complaints were not available.

Reproductive Rights: Couples and individuals have the right to decide freely and responsibly the number, spacing, and timing of their children, and to have the information and means to do so free from discrimination, coercion, and violence. State and territorial governments provided comprehensive sex education, and sexual health and family planning services. Women had access to contraception and skilled medical care, including essential prenatal, obstetric, and postpartum care. Indigenous persons in isolated communities had more difficulty accessing such services than the population as a whole. Cultural factors and language barriers also inhibited use of sexual health and family planning services by indigenous persons, and rates of sexually transmitted diseases and teenage pregnancy among the indigenous population were higher than among the general population.

Discrimination: Women enjoy the same legal rights and status as men, and the law provides for pay equity. According to the Workplace Equality Gender Agency (WEGA), the gender pay gap was 17.5 percent in May with the average weekly ordinary time earnings of women working full-time equal to A$1,252 ($1,165) per week, compared to men who earned an average weekly wage of A$1,518 ($1,412) per week. According to WEGA, the gender pay gap has increased by 1 percentage point since 1995. The law requires organizations with 100 or more employees to establish a workplace program to remove barriers to women's entering and advancing in their organization. The law also prohibits discrimination against employees on the basis of family responsibilities, including breastfeeding.

The HRC received 417 complaints under the Sex Discrimination Act from July 2012 to June. Of 533 complaints that were finalized during this period, 461 included claims on grounds of sex discrimination and 215 included claims on grounds of sexual harassment (some complaints raised multiple grounds). Of the finalized complaints, 165 were terminated, 219 resolved by conciliation, 122 discontinued or withdrawn, and 27 administratively closed.

There were highly organized and effective private and public women's rights organizations at the federal, state, and local levels. The independent federal sex discrimination commissioner, who is part of the HRC, undertakes research, policy, and educational work designed to eliminate gender discrimination. There also is a federal Office for Women, which focuses on reducing violence against women, promoting women's economic security, and enhancing the status of women.

In July the Sex Discrimination Commissioner released an audit of progress towards the implementation of recommendations made by the Review into the Treatment of Women at the Australian Defence Force Academy. The review found the academy was making strides in building a more inclusive place for all its members, including women, and noted the need for an evidence-based sexual ethics program.

Children

Birth Registration: Citizenship is not derived by birth in the country. Children are citizens if at least one parent is a citizen or permanent resident at the time of the child's birth. Children born in the country to parents who are not citizens or permanent residents acquire citizenship on their 10th birthday if they have lived most of their life in the country. Births generally were registered promptly.

Child Abuse: State and territorial child protection agencies investigate and institute prosecutions of persons for child neglect or abuse. All states and territories have laws or guidelines that require members of certain designated professions to report suspected child abuse or neglect. The federal government's role in the prevention of child abuse is limited to funding research, carrying out education campaigns, developing an action plan against the commercial exploitation of children, and funding community-based parenting programs.

According to the Australian Institute of Health and Welfare, there were approximately 37,700 children in substantiated abuse or neglect cases in the 2011-12 fiscal year. This represented approximately one in 135 children under age 18.

Forced and Early Marriage: The legal minimum age of marriage is 18 years for both boys and girls. A person who is between 16 and 18 years may apply to a judge or magistrate in a state or territory for an order authorizing his or her marriage to a person who has attained 18 years of age; however, the marriage of a person under age 18 requires parental or guardian consent. Two persons under age 18 may not marry each other. While no statistics were available, reports of marriages involving a person under age 18 were rare.

Harmful Traditional Practices: Female genital mutilation/cutting (FGM/C) is a crime under the laws of all states and territories, and medical policy prohibits the practice. While the number of residents born in countries where the practice is common was growing, there were very few reports of FGM/C during the year. In September 2012 in Sydney, authorities charged a local Islamic leader, a retired nurse, the girls' parents, and four additional female relatives with performing FGM/C on two young girls, ages six and seven at the time, in the state of New South Wales between October 2010 and July 2012. On July 31, a ninth person was charged in relation to the case. Court proceedings continued as of November.

In April the government held a national summit on FGM/C and subsequently announced a National Compact on Female Genital Mutilation to reinforce and build upon existing efforts. On July 21, the government announced A$1 million ($930,000) in funding for 15 new projects aimed at ending FGM/C.

Sexual Exploitation of Children: The law provides for penalties of up to 25 years' imprisonment for commercial sexual exploitation of children. There were documented cases of children under age 18 engaged in prostitution.

The law prohibits citizens and residents from engaging in, facilitating, or benefiting from sexual activity with children under age 16 overseas, and it provides for a maximum sentence of 17 years' imprisonment upon conviction. The government continued its awareness campaign to deter child sex tourism through the distribution of materials to citizens and residents traveling overseas.

The legal age for consensual sex is 16 in the Australian Capital Territory, New South Wales, the Northern Territory, Victoria, and Western Australia, and 17 in Tasmania and South Australia. In Queensland the age of consent for anal sex is 18, while the age of consent for all other sexual acts is 16. Maximum penalties for violations vary across jurisdictions. Defenses include reasonable grounds for believing that the alleged victim was above the legal age of consent and situations in which the two persons are close in age.

All states and territories criminalize the possession, production, and distribution of child pornography. Maximum penalties for these offenses range from four to 21 years' imprisonment. Federal laws criminalize using a "carriage service" (for example, the internet) for the purpose of possessing, producing, and supplying child pornography. The maximum penalty for these offenses is 10 years' imprisonment and/or a fine of A$275,000 ($255,750). Federal law allows suspected pedophiles to be tried in the country regardless of where the crime is committed. The AFP worked with its international partners to identify and charge persons involved in the online exploitation of children.

The government largely continued federal emergency intervention measures initiated in 2007 to combat child sexual abuse in 73 Aboriginal communities in the Northern Territory. These measures included emergency bans on sales of alcohol and pornography, restrictions on the payment of welfare benefits in cash, linkage of support payments to school attendance, and medical examinations for all indigenous children under age 16 in the Northern Territory. Parliament extended most of the intervention measures through 2022.

While public reaction to the intervention remained generally positive, some Aboriginal activists asserted there was inadequate consultation and that the measures were racially discriminatory, since nonindigenous persons in the Northern Territory were not initially subject to such restrictions.

International Child Abductions: The country is a party to the 1980 Hague Convention on the Civil Aspects of International Child Abduction. For information see the Department of State's report on compliance at www.travel.state.gov/abduction/resources/congressreport/congressreport_4308.html, as well as country-specific information at http://travel.state.gov/abduction/country/country_6197.html.

Anti-Semitism

According to the 2011 census, the country's Jewish community numbered 97,300 persons. During the 12-month period ending in September 2013, the Executive Council of Australian Jewry, an NGO, recorded 657 anti-Semitic incidents, compared with 543 during the previous 12 months. These incidents included physical and verbal assaults, such as Jewish persons walking to and from synagogues being pelted with eggs; vandalism; and harassment.

In October five Jewish adults allegedly were assaulted in Sydney during a suspected anti-Semitic confrontation that reportedly resulted in the hospitalization of some of the victims. Authorities arrested and charged two minors and two adults over the incident, with legal proceedings and a police investigation continuing as of November. Political, religious, and community leaders widely condemned the alleged attack. Subsequent reporting indicated that the Jewish individuals may have been a "target of opportunity" for the attackers – who were reportedly seeking to instigate an altercation motivated more by generally xenophobic attitudes and not specially looking for Jewish people – when they encountered the Jewish group and initiated the alleged altercation.

Trafficking in Persons

See the Department of State's *Trafficking in Persons Report* at www.state.gov/j/tip.

Persons with Disabilities

The law prohibits discrimination against persons with physical, sensory, intellectual, and mental disabilities in employment; education; access to premises; access to air travel and other forms of transport; provision of goods, services (including health services) and facilities; accommodation; purchase of land; activities of clubs and associations; sport; and the administration of federal laws and programs. The government effectively enforced the law.

The disability discrimination commissioner, who is part of the HRC, promotes compliance with federal laws that prohibit discrimination against persons with disabilities. The commissioner also promotes implementation and enforcement of state laws that require equal access to buildings and otherwise protect the rights of persons with disabilities, including ensuring equal access to communications and information. The law also provides for mediation by the HRC of discrimination complaints, authorizes fines against violators, and awards damages to victims of discrimination.

Schools are required to comply with the Disability Discrimination Act, and children with disabilities generally attended school. The federal government's Better Start initiative provided up to A$12,000 ($11,160) in funding for early intervention services and treatment for eligible children with disabilities. The government's More Support for Students with Disabilities initiative allocated A$300 million ($279 million) in additional funding for 2012, 2013, and 2014. The government also cooperated with state and territorial governments that ran programs to assist students with disabilities.

The HRC's annual report stated that 793 complaints citing 1,843 alleged grounds of discrimination were filed under the Disability Discrimination Act from July 2012 to June. Of these, 33 percent related to employment, and 34 percent involved the provision of goods and services. The HRC resolved 961 complaints during the period, including 424 through conciliation.

In July the government launched a national disability insurance program, Disability Care Australia, and the federal budget allocated A$14.3 billion ($13.3 billion) over seven years to the program. It was estimated that 460,000 persons with disabilities would be eligible to benefit from the program by the time it is fully operational in 2019. The first stage of the implementation began in July and was estimated to benefit 26,000 persons with disabilities.

In May the High Court upheld a December 2012 ruling by a lower court that found the Business Services Wage Assessment Tool – an instrument used by disability organizations to determine wages – discriminated against workers with intellectual disabilities. Subsequently, the government appealed to the HRC for a three-year exemption from the Disability Discrimination Act to continue using the instrument "while alternative wage setting arrangements are considered, devised, and/or established and implemented." A decision remained pending as of November.

In July a senate inquiry into "involuntary coerced sterilization of people with disabilities in Australia" made 28 recommendations, including: independent representation for persons with disabilities, establishment of a commonwealth special medical procedures advisory committee, legislation prohibiting the performance or procurement of unauthorized sterilization procedures, and better medical workforce training.

National/Racial/Ethnic Minorities

According to its annual report, the HRC received 500 complaints under the Racial Discrimination Act, citing 997 alleged grounds of discrimination. Of these, 25 percent involved employment, 29 percent involved provision of goods and services, and 27 percent alleged "racial hatred." During this period the HRC resolved 453 complaints, including 189 through conciliation.

In February a prominent journalist was racially abused on a Sydney bus in front of his young daughter. In August a woman was issued a sixth-month good behavior bond (i.e., a "probationary sentence") in relation to the racial abuse of an Asian school student on a Sydney bus in April.

Indigenous People

According to the 2011 census, Aboriginals and Torres Strait Islanders numbered approximately 548,370 persons, or 2.5 percent of the total population.

Indigenous ownership of land was predominately in nonurban areas. Indigenous-owned or controlled land comprised approximately 20 percent of the country's area (excluding native title lands) and nearly 50 percent of the land in the Northern Territory. The National Native Title Tribunal resolves native land title applications through mediation and acts as an arbitrator in cases where the parties cannot reach agreement about proposed mining or other development of land. Under a 2002 High Court ruling, native title rights do not extend to mineral or petroleum resources and, in cases where leaseholder rights and native title rights are in conflict, leaseholder rights prevail but do not extinguish native title rights.

The Indigenous Land Corporation is a special account of A$1 billion ($930 million) that provides a continuing source of funds for indigenous persons to acquire or manage land for the benefit of indigenous Australians. It receives a minimum annual payment of A$45 million ($41.85 million) from the federal government. It is separate from the National Native Title Tribunal and is not for payment of compensation to indigenous persons for loss of land or to titleholders for return of land to indigenous persons.

As part of the intervention to address child sexual abuse in Northern Territory indigenous communities (see section 6, Children), in 2007 the government took control of 64 indigenous communities through five-year land leases. The Stronger Futures in the Northern Territory plan begun in 2012 repealed the emergency response and provided for negotiation of voluntary long-term leases. Stronger

Futures intended to invest $A3.4 billion ($3.16 billion) between 2012 and 2022 to address indigenous disadvantage.

In March parliament unanimously passed an act of recognition intended to build momentum for a future referendum for constitutional recognition of indigenous people. The new government supported constitutional recognition of indigenous people and indicated it is committed to working toward a referendum to achieve this aim. The portfolio of indigenous affairs was granted cabinet-level status, and indigenous policy coordination shifted to the Department of Prime Minister and Cabinet.

During a visit to the country in May, the UN special rapporteur on the rights of indigenous peoples supported moves to recognize indigenous people in the constitution.

The government expressed a commitment to "closing the gap" on indigenous inequalities, and since 2008 the prime minister has reported to parliament the progress on this effort at the beginning of each year. The 2013 report found targets for early childhood education, infant mortality, and completion of year 12 education were on track to be achieved. The report indicated that progress had been made on a target to halve the gap in reading, writing, and numeracy between indigenous and nonindigenous students within a decade.

According to the ABS, in 2012 indigenous adults were 15 times more likely than nonindigenous adults to be imprisoned and comprised 27 percent of the prison population. In a 2011 report, ABS found that life expectancy for indigenous men was estimated to be 67.2 years, compared with 78.7 years for nonindigenous men; life expectancy for indigenous women was estimated to be 72.9 years, compared with 82.6 years for nonindigenous women; and the indigenous unemployment rate was 16 percent, compared with approximately 5 percent for the nonindigenous population.

The Productivity Commission's 2012 Indigenous Expenditure Report estimated that total direct indigenous expenditure in 2010-11 was A$25.4 billion ($23.6 billion). This resulted in spending of A$44,128 ($41,039) per indigenous citizen compared to A$19,589 ($18, 217) for other citizens. The report found that the difference was due to "greater intensity of service use" and "additional costs of providing services."

The National Congress of Australia's First Peoples is the national representative body for Aboriginals and Torres Strait Islanders. From July 2012 it was designated to receive A$29.2 million ($27.16 million) over five years from the federal government. The HRC has an Aboriginal and Torres Strait Islander social justice commissioner.

Societal Abuses, Discrimination, and Acts of Violence Based on Sexual Orientation and Gender Identity

No laws criminalize consensual same-sex sexual conduct between adults. Discrimination on the basis of sexual orientation and gender identity is prohibited by law in a wide range of areas, including in employment, housing, family law, taxes, child support, immigration, pensions, aged care, and social security.

The HRC received 16 complaints of discrimination based on sexual orientation from July 2012 through June. Information on resolution of the complaints was not available.

In June the Sex Discrimination Act was amended to provide additional protections against discrimination on the basis of sexual orientation, gender identity, and intersex status.

Other Societal Violence or Discrimination

Federal and various state laws prohibit discrimination on the ground of HIV-positive status. The government generally enforced these laws effectively. The HRC reviews complaints of discrimination on the ground of HIV/AIDS status under the category of disability-related complaints, but a specific breakdown of HIV/AIDS-related cases was not available. There were no known reports of violence against persons based on HIV/AIDS status.

Section 7. Worker Rights

a. Freedom of Association and the Right to Collective Bargaining

The law, including related regulations and statutory instruments, protects the rights of workers, including public servants, to associate freely domestically and internationally and also protects against antiunion discrimination. Federal, state, and territorial laws protect workers' rights to organize, conduct legal strikes, and bargain collectively. Labor laws protect citizens, permanent residents, and migrant workers. The government effectively enforced applicable laws.

Under the law workers are free to join or decline to join industrial associations. The law prohibits discrimination against individuals for membership or nonmembership in a union and provides for reinstatement of workers fired for union activity. Nationally, employers and other unions have the right to challenge changes to union "eligibility rules," which essentially outline the types of employees the union may represent.

The law provides for the right to strike but confines strikes to the period when unions are negotiating a new enterprise agreement and specifies that strikes must concern matters under negotiation. This is known as "protected action." Protected action provides employers, employees, and unions with legal immunity from claims of losses incurred by industrial action. The deadline to lodge an unfair dismissal claim was extended from 14 days to 21 days, and the time to lodge a general protections claim was reduced from 60 to 21 days. This alignment was made to correct alleged misuse of the general protections provisions by those who had missed the unfair dismissal claim deadline. The law subjects strikers to penalties for taking industrial action during the life of an agreement and contains secondary action (e.g., sympathy strike) provisions. Federal and state laws regulate strikes in essential services, such as law enforcement, air-traffic control, and sanitation. The law permits the government to stop strikes judged to have an "adverse effect" on the employer or damage third parties, but this provision was not used during the year. Industrial action must be authorized by a secret ballot of employees; unions complained that this requirement was unduly time consuming and expensive to implement.

With regard to collective bargaining, the law requires that employers act in "good faith" when a majority of employees want a collective agreement and enables low-paid workers to engage in multi-employer "good faith bargaining." A bargaining agent may represent either side in the process.

An enterprise agreement – a collective agreement made at an enterprise level between employers and employees – cannot override relevant laws. For example, an enterprise agreement cannot include "a term that confers an entitlement or remedy in relation to unfair dismissal before the employee has completed the minimum employment period."

The Fair Work Commission is an independent industrial relations management institution. Its functions include determining minimum wages and employment conditions, and dispute resolution. There is a national safety net of minimum employment standards. On July 1, mandatory employer contributions to retirement funds were lifted from 9 percent of a worker's income to 9.25 percent and were scheduled to gradually increase to 12 percent by 2019. These contributions are not drawn from a worker's wage.

By law union officials have the right to enter workplaces if they hold right-of-entry permits granted by the Fair Work Commission. Written notice is generally required to enter a workplace and should be provided no less than 24 hours and no more than 14 days before the proposed visit. A permit holder may enter premises to hold discussions with one or more employees. Eligibility to enter premises is not dependent on whether a union is party to an award or enterprise agreement, but rather on whether a union covers the work of a particular employee.

Unions carried out their functions free from government or political control. Almost all unions were affiliated with the Australian Council of Trade Unions (ACTU). Workers exercised the right to associate freely with generally few constraints, but some obstacles remained. For example, in New South Wales, registration of a union may be canceled if a strike has a substantially adverse effect on public service or defies an order of the New South Wales Industrial Relations Commission.

b. Prohibition of Forced or Compulsory Labor

The law explicitly prohibits forced or compulsory labor, but there were some reports of foreign nationals who came to the country for temporary work being subjected to forced labor by employers or labor agencies in such sectors as agriculture, cleaning, construction, hospitality, manufacturing, and domestic service.

Also see the Department of State's *Trafficking in Persons Report* at www.state.gov/j/tip.

c. Prohibition of Child Labor and Minimum Age for Employment

There is no federally mandated minimum age of employment, but state-imposed compulsory educational requirements, enforced by state educational authorities, effectively prevented most children from joining the work force full time until they were age 17. Federal, state, and territorial governments effectively monitored and enforced a network of laws, which varied among jurisdictions, governing the minimum age for leaving school, claiming unemployment benefits, and engaging in specified occupations. The ACTU also monitored adherence to these laws.

d. Acceptable Conditions of Work

The Fair Work Act of 2013 includes an antibullying provision that enables workers who are bullied at work to apply to the Fair Work Commission for an order to stop the bullying. Another change made by the act was to enable workers who are pregnant to transfer to a safe job regardless of their time in employment.

Effective July 1, the Fair Work Commission increased the national minimum wage for adults working full time (38 hours per week) by 2.6 percent from A$606.40 ($563.95) per week to A$622.20 ($578.65) per week, based on a minimum hourly rate of A$16.37 ($15.22). There was no official poverty-level income figure, but the minimum wage, combined with welfare payments, was intended to provide a decent standard of living for a worker and family. Although a formal minimum wage exists, most workers received higher wages through enterprise agreements or individual contracts. Above-minimum-wage classifications apply to certain trades and professions. The law requires equal pay for equal work.

A taxpayer-funded Paid Parental Leave Scheme pays the minimum wage rate for up to 18 weeks to workers who have worked for at least 330 hours during at least 10 of the 13 months prior to the birth or adoption of a child.

Under the law maximum weekly hours are 38 plus "reasonable" additional hours (determined according to the law, taking into account factors such as an employee's health, family responsibilities, ability to claim overtime, pattern of hours in the industry, and amount of notice given). The law provides for paid annual holidays and premium pay for overtime. Industry standards or awards mandate rest periods and overtime pay. Migrant worker visas require that employers respect these protections and provide bonds to cover health insurance, worker's compensation insurance, unemployment insurance, and other benefits.

Federal or state occupational health and safety laws apply to every workplace.

The Fair Work Ombudsman provides employers and employees advice about their rights and has authority to investigate employers alleged to have exploited employees unlawfully. The ombudsman also has authority to prosecute employers that do not meet their obligations to workers. Employers can be ordered to compensate employees and are sometimes assessed fines. Between July 2012 and June, the Fair Work Ombudsman recovered A$24.46 million ($22.75 million) on behalf of 17,434 employees. Workers exercised their right to a safe workplace and have recourse to state health and safety commissions, which investigate complaints and order remedial action.

During the past two decades, the percentage of the workforce regarded as temporary workers increased. Temporary workers include both part-time and casual employees. Part-time employees have set hours and the same entitlements as full-time employees. The ABS reported that, as of July, approximately 3.52 million persons (30 percent of the workforce) were employed as part-time workers, of whom 70 percent were women. Casual employees are employed on a daily or hourly wage basis. They do not receive paid annual or sick leave, but the law mandates they receive additional pay to compensate for this.

There were reports that some individuals on so-called 457 employer-sponsored, skilled-worker visas were underpaid and used as a less expensive substitute for Australian workers. In June the Fair Work Ombudsman initiated legal action against a Tasmanian restaurant that allegedly underpaid a chef recruited under a 457 visa by A$88,000 ($81,840) over three years. On June 28, parliament passed the Migration Amendment (Temporary Sponsored Visas) Bill 2013, which requires employers to undertake "labor market testing" before attempting to sponsor 457 visas. On July 1, the Skilled Migration Income Threshold was indexed by 4.8 percent from A$51,400 ($47,802) to A$53,900 ($50,127), in line with the increase in average weekly earnings. This meant that when the market rate annual salary for a position was less than A$53,900 ($50,127), the position could not be nominated under the subclass 457 program.

There were no reports of worker rights abuses in the country's three inhabited dependent territories of Christmas Island, Cocos (Keeling) Islands, and Norfolk Island.